IT'S HARD
TO BE HIP
OVER THIRTY
AND OTHER
TRAGEDIES OF
MARRIED
LIFE

Books by Judith Viorst

The Village Square
Sunday Morning
It's Hard to Be Hip Over Thirty . . . and Other Tragedies of Married Life

IT'S HARD TO BE HIP OVER THIRTY AND OTHER TRAGEDIES OF MARRIED LIFE

BY JUDITH VIORST

AN **NAL** BOOK
THE WORLD
PUBLISHING
COMPANY
NEW YORK AND
CLEVELAND

FIRST PRINTING—NOVEMBER, 1968
SECOND PRINTING—JANUARY, 1969
THIRD PRINTING—FEBRUARY, 1969
FOURTH PRINTING—FEBRUARY, 1969
FIFTH PRINTING—APRIL, 1969

Published by The New American Library, Inc.
in association with The World Publishing Company
2231 West 110th Street, Cleveland, Ohio 44102

Library of Congress Catalog Card Number: 68-56139

Printed in the United States of America

BOOK DESIGN: HERB LUBALIN
ILLUSTRATIONS: JOHN ALCORN

To Milton

I wish to thank Clay Felker, Joanne Goldfarb, Robert Gutwillig, Linda and Michael Halberstam, Robert Lescher, Elizabeth Rubenstein, and Milton Viorst for their moral support, their editorial guidance, and/or their expertise on the subject of marriage.

Contents

The First Years

Marriage and the Families   12
The Honeymoon Is Over   14
A Good Catch   16
Maybe We'll Make It   18
Nice Baby   20

The Years After That

The Suburbs Are Good for the Children   24
The Suburbanites   26
Choices   28
Striking Back   30
It's Hard to Be Hip Over Thirty   32
A Visit From My Mother-In-Law   34
The Other Woman   36
Money   38
The Fix-Up   40
Where Is It Written?   42
Married Is Better   44
The Cocktail Party   46

The Vacation

Getting Ready   50
Aboard the SS France   52
In Deauville   54
In Paris   56
Back Home   58

The Adjustment

Sex Is Not So Sexy Anymore   62
The Divorce   64
Infidelity   66
The Generation Gap   68
True Love   70

The
First
Years

Marriage and the Families

My mother was grateful
He wasn't barefoot.
His mother was grateful
I wasn't pregnant.

My father was grateful
He wasn't a Negro or unemployed.
His father was grateful
I wasn't tubercular or divorced.

My sister was grateful
Her husband was richer and taller.
His sister was grateful
She had a master's degree and a better nose.

My cousin in luggage was grateful
He didn't expect a discount.
His cousin the dentist was grateful
I didn't need root canal.

My aunts and my uncles were grateful
He came from a nice family in New Jersey even though he wore
    sunglasses in the living room which is usually a sign of
    depravity.
His aunts and his uncles were grateful
I came from a nice family in New Jersey even though I lived in
    Greenwich Village which is usually a sign of depravity also.

I should be pleased.

But when I think of the catered wedding in Upper Montclair,
With the roast sirloin of beef dinner,
The souvenir photo album,
And the matches with our names in raised gold letters,
And when I think of the Ronson lighters, the savings bonds, the
    cut glass, and the sugars and creamers both sterling and silver plate,
Then I wish
That they weren't
So grateful.

The Honeymoon Is Over

The honeymoon is over
And he has left for work
Whistling something obvious from La Bohème
And carrying a brown calfskin attaché case
I never dreamed he was capable of owning,
Having started the day
With ten pushups and a cold shower
Followed by a hearty breakfast.

(What do we actually have in common?)

The honeymoon is over
And I am dry-mopping the floor
In a green Dacron dry-mopping outfit from Saks,
Wondering why I'm not dancing in the dark,
Or rejecting princes,
Or hearing people gasp at my one-man show,
My god, so beautiful and so gifted!

(The trouble is I never knew a prince.)

The honeymoon is over
And we find that dining by candlelight makes us squint,
And that all the time
I was letting him borrow my comb and hang up his wet raincoat
        in my closet,
I was really waiting
To stop letting him.
And that all the time
He was saying how he loved my chicken pot pie,
He was really waiting
To stop eating it.

(I guess they call this getting to know each other.)

A Good Catch

Although he is still wearing his college ring,
And driving a white Imperial,
And taking girls to supper clubs where the entire meal is served flambé
Because he still thinks the more flames the better,
Freddie the bachelor
Is what is known in New Jersey as
A good catch.

He has waves in his hair,
Caps on his teeth,
A manicure on his nails,
And what is known in New Jersey as
A nice physique. Also
A clean bill of health,
A great sense of humor,
And a steady job,
With what is known in New Jersey as
Room for advancement. Also
Serious interests
Such as reading and Broadway plays
That are not even musicals.

Although he still remembers the fraternity handshake,
And the football cheers,
And is still singing in girls' ears while dancing
Because someone once told him that singing in ears is sexy,
Freddie the bachelor
Is what is known in New Jersey as
A good catch.

He has cashmere sweaters,
A Danish-modern apartment,
A retirement plan,
And what is known in New Jersey as
Sound investments. Also
A way with children,
Consideration for others,
And what is known in New Jersey as
A good head on his shoulders. Also
Important contacts
Such as a nephew of the Congressman
From Flushing.

And whenever my husband is showing
What is known in New Jersey as no respect
For my mother,
She tells about Freddie the bachelor,
Who never talks back and is such
A good catch.

17

Maybe We'll Make It

If I quit hoping he'll show up with flowers, and
He quits hoping I'll squeeze him an orange, and
I quit shaving my legs with his razor, and
He quits wiping his feet with my face towel, and
We avoid discussions like
Is he really smarter than I am, or simply more glib,
Maybe we'll make it.

If I quit looking to prove that he's hostile, and
He quits looking for dust on the tables, and
I quit inviting Louise with the giggle, and
He quits inviting Jerome with the complex, and
We avoid discussions like
Suppose I died, which one of our friends would he marry,
Maybe we'll make it.

We've fully examined James Reston, the war,
John Updike, religion, the Renaissance, CORE,
And on all major issues we're for and against
The same things.
Yet somehow we've managed to not miss a fight.
He tells me there's nothing to nosh on at night.
I tell him that no one can sleep with a light in her eyes,
Not to mention
He takes too much time in the bathroom. But

If I quit clearing the plates while he's eating, and
He quits clearing his throat while I'm speaking, and
I quit implying I could have done better, and
He quits implying he wishes I had, and
We avoid discussions like
Does his mother really love him, or is she simply one of those
    over-possessive, devouring women who can't let go,
Maybe we'll make it.

Nice Baby

Last year I talked about black humor and the impact of the common
          market on the European economy and
Threw clever little cocktail parties in our discerningly eclectic
          living room
With the Spanish rug and the hand-carved Chinese chest and the lucite
          chairs and
Was occasionally hungered after by highly placed men in
          communications, but
This year we have a nice baby
And pablum drying on our Spanish rug,
And I talk about nursing versus sterilization
While the men in communications
Hunger elsewhere.

Last year I studied flamenco and had my ears pierced and
Served an authentic fondue on the Belgian marble table of our
     discerningly eclectic dining area, but
This year we have a nice baby
And Spock on the second shelf of our Chinese chest,
And instead of finding myself I am doing my best
To find a sitter
For the nice baby banging the Belgian marble with his cup
While I heat the oven up
For the TV dinners.

Last year I had a shampoo and set every week and
Slept an unbroken sleep beneath the Venetian chandelier of our
          discerningly eclectic bedroom, but
This year we have a nice baby,
And Gerber's strained bananas in my hair,
And gleaming beneath the Venetian chandelier,
A diaper pail, a portacrib, and him,
A nice baby, drooling on our antique satin spread
While I smile and say how nice. It is often said
That motherhood is very maturing.

The
Years
After
That

The Suburbs
Are Good for the Children

The suburbs are good for the children.
A child needs clean air and a yard
And a barbecue pit and a gaslight.
We certainly tried very hard
To buy a home next to a Negro
Or other race, color, or creed.
God knows we adore integration,
But everyone knows children need
The feeling of roots that a rec room
And genuine oak-paneled den
Can offer to split-level households
In places called Bonnie Brae Glen,
Where wall-to-wall fires are burning
In family rooms floored in parquet
And bread bakes in eye-level ovens
Designed by G.E. in dove-gray,
Where civic clubs meet every Friday
And girl scouts watch birds in the park
And even if you went out looking
You couldn't get raped after dark.
With four walk-in closets to walk in,
Three bushes, two shrubs, and one tree,
The suburbs are good for the children,
But no place for grown-ups to be.

The Suburbanites

They love it here.
They say
New York is a dirty town. Full of
    sex fiends,
    and dope fiends,
    and irresponsible people crossing against the light,
    ruthless people writing television commercials for money,
    hostile people riding the IRT.
    (You could sit forever in Chock Full O'Nuts,
    they say,
    and never meet a person you could trust.)
And New York is full of
    pop artists,
    op artists,
    and avant-garde people who know which Westerns to like,
    sneaky people hiding behind dark glasses,
    heartless people ignoring screams of help.
    (You could drop dead in the middle of Times Square,
    they say,
    and no one would even offer a glass of water.)
And New York is full of
    litterbugs,
    the Mafia,
    aggressive women going to work in hats,
    nervous people with psychiatrists on Central Park West,
    wicked people living with other wicked people to whom they
        are not married,
    emancipated people thinking it's smart to talk back to
        their mothers,
    greedy slumlords,
    sinister foreigners,
    and uppity neighbors.
    (You could live your whole life on East Sixty-fifth,
    they say,
    and the Welcome Wagon would never bring a cake.)

Choices

We've met the fun couples
Who own works of art
That are strawberry malteds in plaster,
And watch television
Only to see the commercials,
And use words like life style and panache.

And we've met the boycott-the-supermarket people
Who oppose certain conservative instant puddings
And support certain progressive canned vegetables
In addition to voter registration, busing, and immediate withdrawal.

And we've met the above-reproach crowd
Who are signed up for
Cancer,
Heart disease,
Stroke,
A booth at the annual book fair,
And he goes to sewer meetings in tweed jackets
With leather elbow patches
While she exchanges recipes
At brunches.

And we've met the social leaders
Who know how to act at horse shows,
And their ancestors always come from the British Isles.

And we've met the self-improvers
Who buy quality paperbacks,
Season tickets to theaters in the round,
And Brentano reproductions.

And we can't decide
Who we want them to think
We are.

Striking Back

When a husband tells a wife
Stop screaming at the children
And he isn't crazy about the drapes
And why doesn't she learn where Thailand is
And maybe she should cut her hair
(All of which, needless to say, are implicit attacks on her
Intelligence,
Taste,
Desirability,
And maternal instincts)
A wife
Can only
Strike back.

So sometimes I try
My mother's technique
Which is silence for a week,
A brooding stare into the ruined future,
And no rouge for that look of
You are making me so miserable you are giving me
A fatal illness.

It occasionally works.

And sometimes I try
Weeping, cursing, expressions of bitter remorse,
And don't ever expect to see the children again,
Which I often follow with phone calls pricing suites
At expensive hotels.

I've had limited success.

There is also
The psychoanalytic confrontation
Which entails informing him
(More, of course, in sorrow than in anger)
That his sadistic treatment of those who love him is a sign of
        unconscious feelings of inadequacy and
He needs help.

I've dropped this approach.

But there is always
Total recall
During which all the wrongs he has done me since first we met
Are laid before him.
And when this is combined
With refusing to go to the Greenberg's annual costume party,
Tossing and moaning in my sleep,
And threatening to commit suicide, take a lover, and drop out of the
        PTA because why try to save the school system when my entire
        universe is falling apart,
I start to feel
I'm really
Striking back.

It's Hard to Be Hip Over Thirty

All around New York
Perfect girls with hairpieces and fishnet jumpsuits
Sit in their art nouveau apartments
Discussing things like King Kong
With people like Rudolph Nureyev.

Meanwhile, the rest of us,
Serving Crispy Critters to grouchy three-year-olds
And drinking our Metrecal,
Dream of snapping our fingers to the music
If only we knew when to snap.

But it's hard to be hip over thirty
When everyone else is nineteen,
When the last dance we learned was the Lindy
And the last we heard, girls who looked like Barbra Streisand
Were trying to do something about it.

We long to be kicky and camp—but
The maid only comes once a week.
And since we have to show up for the car pool,
Orgiastic pot parties with cool Negroes who say "funky" and "man"
Seem rather impractical.

The Love Song of J. Alfred Prufrock,
Which we learned line by line long ago,
Doesn't swing, we are told, on East Tenth Street,
Where all the perfect girls are switched-on or tuned-in or miscegenated,
But never over thirty
Trying hard
To be hip.

A Visit From My Mother-In-Law

My mother-in-law
Comes to visit
With her own apron,
Her own jar of Nescafé,
And the latest news.

Uncle Leo,
She's sorry to say,
Is divorcing Aunt Pearl,
Whose sister Bernice
Is having
A nervous breakdown.
The week
That they spent in Miami
It rained every day,
And her health,
Though she isn't complaining,
Has never been worse.
The lady upstairs
With the limp
Was attacked in broad daylight,
And Seymour her nephew
Has cataracts, flu,
And no job.
My husband,
She thinks she should mention,
Looks thin as a rail,
And the children,
It hurts her to hear,
Are coughing again.
Belle's son,
Only forty years old,
Dropped dead Friday morning,
And don't even bother
To ask
About Cousin Rose.

I don't think I will.

The Other Woman

The other woman
Never smells of Ajax or Spaghetti-O,
And was bored with Bob Dylan
A year before we had heard of him,
And is a good sport about things like flat tires and no hot water,
Because it's easier to be a good sport
When you're not married.

The other woman
Never has tired blood,
And can name the best hotels in Acapulco
As readily as we can name detergents,
And wears a chiffon peignoir instead of a corduroy bathrobe,
Because it's easier to try harder
When you're not married.

The other woman
Never has to look at Secret Squirrel,
And spends her money on fun furs
While we are spending ours on obstetricians,
And can make a husband feel that he is wanted,
Because it's easier to want a husband
When you're not married.

Money

Once I aspired to
Humble black turtleneck sweaters
And spare unheated rooms
With the Kama Sutra, a few madrigals, and
Great literature and philosophy.

Once I considered money
Something to be against
On the grounds that
Credit cards,
Installment-plan buying,
And a joint checking account
Could never coexist with
Great literature and philosophy.

Once I believed
That the only kind of marriage I could respect
Was a spiritual relationship
Between two wonderfully spiritual human beings
Who would never argue about money
Because they would be too busy arguing about
Great literature and philosophy.

I changed my mind,
Having discovered that

Spiritual is hard without the cash
To pay the plumber to unstop the sink
And pay a lady to come clean and iron
So every other Friday I can think about
Great literature and philosophy.

No one ever offers us a choice
Between the Kama Sutra and a yacht.
We're always selling out for diaper service
And other drab necessities that got ignored in
Great literature and philosophy.

A jug of wine, a loaf of bread, and thou
No longer will suffice. I must confess
My consciousness is frequently expanded
By Diners' Club, American Express, and things undreamed of in
Great literature and philosophy.

I saw us walking hand-in-hand through life,
But now it's clear we really need two cars.
I looked with such contempt at power mowers,
And now, alas, that power mower's ours.
It seems I'm always reaching for my charge plates,
When all I'd planned to reach for were the stars,
Great literature and philosophy.

The Fix-Up

I have this friend Muriel who is attractive and intelligent and
        terribly understanding and loyal and
My husband has this friend Ralph who is handsome and witty and
        essentially very sincere and
Since they weren't engaged or even tacitly committed
The least we could do, I said, is fix them up,
So I cooked this very nice boned chicken breasts with lemon-cream
        sauce and
Put on a little Herb Alpert in the background and
Before Muriel came I told Ralph how she was attractive and intelligent
        and terribly understanding and loyal and
After Muriel came I drew out Ralph to show how he was witty and
        very sincere and
When dinner was over my husband and I did the dishes
Leaving Ralph and Muriel to get acquainted
With a little Petula Clark in the background and
We listened while they discovered that they both loved Mel Brooks
        and hated Los Angeles and agreed that the Supremes had lost
        their touch and
He insisted on taking her home even though she lived in the opposite
        direction and
The next day he phoned to ask is that what I call attractive, after which
She phoned to ask is that what I call sincere
And from now on
I cook lemon-cream sauce
For young marrieds.

41

Where Is It Written?

Where is it written
That husbands get twenty-five-dollar lunches and invitations to South
    America for think conferences while
Wives get Campbell's black bean soup and a trip to the firehouse with
    the first grade and
Where is it written
That husbands get to meet beautiful lady lawyers and beautiful lady
    professors of Ancient History and beautiful sculptresses and
    heiresses and poetesses while
Wives get to meet the checker with the acne at the Safeway and
Where is it written
That husbands get a nap and the Super Bowl on Sundays while
Wives get to help color in the coloring book and
Where is it written
That husbands get ego gratification, emotional support, and hot tea in
    bed for ten days when they have the sniffles while
Wives get to give it to them?

And if a wife should finally decide
Let him take the shoes to the shoemaker and the children to the
    pediatrician and the dog to the vet while she takes up something
    like brain surgery or transcendental meditation,
Where is it written
That she always has to feel
Guilty?

Married Is Better

There are those of us who gave up a promising career
As assistant to the editorial assistant to the editor
Or secretary to the private secretary of the executive producer,
And a glittering social life
Of boîtes, soirées, and happenings,
And romance in the form of
Brief encounters, moonlight and love songs, I can't live without you,
And so forth,
Because, as someone once put it,
Married is better.

Married is better
Than sitting on a blanket in Nantucket
Where you get blotches and a red nose instead of adorable freckles and
    golden brown,
Hoping that someone with whom you would not be caught dead
From September to June
Will invite you to dinner,

And it is better
Than riding a double chair lift up at Stowe
On your way to an expert trail and you're a beginner,
Hoping the fellow for whom you are risking your life
Will invite you to dinner.
And one night, when you land at Kennedy, and no one is there to meet
     you except your parents
And you suddenly realize that you never saw the Parthenon because you
     were too busy looking around for a Greek god,
You also suddenly realize
Married is better.

And married is better
Than an affair with a marvelous man
Who would leave his wife immediately except that she would slash her
     wrists and the children would cry.
So instead you drink his Scotch in your living room and never meet his
     friends because they might become disillusioned or tell,
And when it's your birthday it's his evening with the in-laws,
And when it's his birthday he can't even bring home your present
(Because of the slashed wrists and the crying and all),
And even though you have his body and soul while his wife only has his
     laundry and the same name,
You somehow begin to suspect
Married is better.

And married is better
Than the subway plus a crosstown bus every morning,
And tuna on toasted cheese bread, no lettuce, at Schrafft's,
And a bachelor-girl apartment with burlap and foam rubber and a few
     droll touches like a Samurai sword in the bathroom,
And going to the movies alone,
And worrying that one morning you'll wake up and discover you're an
     older woman,
And always projecting wholesome sexuality combined with
     independence, femininity, and tons of outside interests,
And never for a minute letting on
That deep in your heart you believe
Married is better.

The Cocktail Party

The hostess is passing the sour-cream dip and the carrots, and
The husband is mixing up something with rum in the blender, and
The mothers are finishing teething and starting on ear aches, and
The ones with the tan are describing their trip to St. Thomas, and
The fellow they swore was funnier than Joey Bishop
Is discussing tax breaks
With the fellow they swore was funnier than Mort Sahl,
and
The hostess is passing the eggs with the mayonnaise-curry, and
The husband is being risqué with a blonde in the foyer, and
The mothers are finishing ear aches and starting on day camps, and
The one who can play the piano is playing Deep Purple, and
The fellow they swore was smarter than David Susskind
Is discussing field goals
With the fellow they swore was smarter than Max Lerner,
and
The hostess is passing the heat-and-serve pigs-in-a-blanket, and
The husband is passing out cold on the coats in the bedroom, and
The mothers are finishing day camps and starting on sex play, and
The one on the diet is saying she's not even hungry, and
The fellow they swore was cuter than Warren Beatty
Is discussing drain pipes
With the fellow they swore was cuter than Michael Caine,
and
I'm not as out of place
As I wish I were.

The
Vacation

Getting Ready

Every summer
I go to places like Truro
With the three children, my husband, and a mother's helper
Who is always a lithe, bronze, sexually emancipated nineteen-year-old
Who is always playing tennis with my husband
While I sweep out the sand,
Remove bathing suits from the garbage disposal,
And entertain large numbers of strangers
With marinated artichokes and gin.

But this summer
I have given the kids
To an overweight, sexually inhibited, sixty-year-old mother's helper—
My mother.
And, having persuaded myself
That miniskirts and varicose veins are not, in all cases,
Mutually exclusive,
I have purchased a complete love-in drop-out wardrobe
From the suburban branch of Franklin Simon.

I have, in addition,
Acquired the conditional perfect tense from Berlitz,
Stomach muscles from yoga,
Long hair from a second cousin who gets it wholesale,
And, from impeccable sources on the New Left,
The latest views on riots, heart transplants, our suicidal foreign policy,
     and Jewish novelists.

I am, I feel, ready at last for France.
I only hope that France is ready for me.

51

Aboard The SS France

I was expecting
Gay flirtations on the promenade deck,
Smoldering glances across the mid-morning bouillon,
An improper proposal or two
Deftly turned away with regretful sighs.
But no one asked.

So I sit in the smoking room of the SS France
Showing pictures of the kids
To a White Plains widow with heartburn
While some very clean teachers on grants
Discuss the cost of living
With a dry-goods merchant from Nice
And several men who look like my Uncle Max
Are forgetting the bad backs and the high blood pressure
Long enough to do the bossa nova
With clerk-typists in Macy's pants suits.

And though I have tried
The heated swimming pool,
The movies, the music, the champagne,
The foie gras de Siorac à la gelée au Xérès,
Not to mention one gala,
One spectacular,
And plenty of ping-pong,
I keep finding
Exchange students singing Old MacDonald,
Ladies in imitation Puccis comparing laxatives,
And countless adolescents named Stevie and Marv.

So the next time I want a fleeting moment of passion
With the wind and the salt spray in my hair
And someone bitter but basically worthwhile
Laying his soul bare
Beside me, at the rail,
I think I'll take the Hudson River Day Line.

53

In Deauville

In Deauville
Everyone but us
Is a fading French actress,
An Italian polo player,
An obscene American novelist,
Or a pretender to some throne,
All of whom are exchanging quips and barbs
And other chic things
With heiresses, scions, magnates,
Doomed but gallant contessas,
And dégagé Parisians in maroon ascots and four-inch sideburns.

In Deauville
Everyone but us
Is playing chemin de fer
The way my mother plays in the Tuesday gin club,
And buying horses
The way my father buys a good cigar
And telling the waiter the champagne smells of cork
With the assurance of those
Who have never saved trading stamps
Or attended a swim club cook-out.

And even if we had arrived
With an Alfa Romeo,
A yacht,
His and her dinner clothes by Pierre Cardin,
And a handwritten introduction from Francoise Sagan,
They would still know
We did not belong
In Deauville.

In Paris

I am (where else?) at the Deux Magots
Moodily drinking a pernod
And trying to think thoughts
Jean-Paul Sartre would respect
And trying to convey the impression
That I am someone with a rich full inner life
Instead of someone
Who gets palpitations
When the washer-dryer breaks down.

We've chosen a très charmant hotel
With a w.c. in the hall and an elevator
That was designed by Marat or de Sade.
And when I gaze at Notre Dame and the Arch of Triumph,
Having cultural insights about Gothic architecture and the vanity of
        power and similar transcendent topics,
You could think I was someone who subscribes to The Kenyon Review,
Instead of someone
Who reads
Can This Marriage Be Saved?

Meanwhile, the Georges V ladies
Are getting the facials and comb-outs every morning.
After which they put on their little Chanels
And visit Hermès, the Dior boutique, and other crass, insensitive places.
And all those people with Kodaks
Are snapping more people with Kodaks
At the Eiffel Tower and other readily recognizable places.
And a thousand flower children
Are walking their beards and bells
Barefoot down the Boulevard Saint-Michel
And other psychedelic places.
And whom can I identify with now?

So I'm here (why not?) at the Deux Magots
Buying Le Monde in French although
I feel more secure with the Herald Tribune in English.
And in my heart of hearts I know
I should have come here years ago
When I had a total grasp of The Stranger and Gérard Philippe
        and the difference between a Cézanne and a Matisse without even
        peeking at the signatures,
And when I had never heard of Whip 'n Chill or contour diapers or
        term insurance,
And when I would have been someone with unplumbed hidden depths,
Instead of someone
With color television
In the rumpus room.   57

Back Home

The French do not understand
Ronald Reagan for President,
Or peanut butter and jelly sandwiches for lunch.
And I do not understand
The franc,
The Renault R-10,
Or the liver.

The French do not understand
The Peck & Peck girl,
Or paper bags.
And I do not understand
Their telephones,
Their Général,
Or their Gauloises bleues.

But today
When I was defrosting the refrigerator,
And telling the laundry no starch,
And asking the butcher to cut off all the fat,
And wiping fingerpaints from the floor of the co-op nursery,
And catching up on
Poverty,
Escalation,
Crime in the streets,
The crisis in the schools,
H. Rap Brown,
Mary Worth,
And the Beautiful People,
I find
I do not understand
America.

The
Adjustment

Sex Is Not So Sexy Anymore

I bring the children one more glass of water.
I rub the hormone night cream on my face.
Then after I complete the isometrics,
I greet my husband with a warm embrace,

A vision in my long-sleeved flannel nightgown
And socks (because my feet are always freezing),
Gulping tranquilizers for my nerve ends,
And Triaminic tablets for my wheezing.

Our blue electric blanket's set for toasty.
Our red alarm clock's set at seven-thirty.
I tell him that we owe the grocer plenty.
He tells me that his two best suits are dirty.

Last year I bought him Centaur for his birthday.
(They promised he'd become half-man, half-beast.)
Last year he bought me something black and lacy.
(They promised I'd go mad with lust, at least.)

Instead my rollers clink upon the pillow
And his big toenail scrapes against my skin.
He rises to apply a little Chap Stick.
I ask him to bring back two Bufferin.

Oh somewhere there are lovely little boudoirs
With Porthault sheets and canopies and whips.
He lion-hunts in Africa on weekends.
She measures thirty-three around the hips.

Their eyes engage across the brandy snifters.
He runs his fingers through her Kenneth hair.
The kids are in the other wing with nanny.
The sound of violins is everywhere.

In our house there's the sound of dripping water.
It's raining and he never patched the leak.
He grabs the mop and I get out the bucket.
We both agree to try again next week.

The Divorce

Mark and June
Who were such a perfect match
That everyone used to say how perfect they were
Are getting a divorce, because
He only likes spy movies and Audrey Hepburn movies and movies
      that leave you feeling good and
She only likes early Chaplin movies and movies with subtitles
      and movies that leave you feeling rotten and
He thinks Maria Montessori is a fascist and
She thinks Will and Ariel Durant have an unwholesome relationship and
He says she should pick up his socks and drop them in the hamper and
She says he should.

Mark is keeping the Honda
And June is keeping the Mercedes and the Picasso lithographs
As well as the Early American hutch table that they bought for a
      song in Philadelphia, because
He says it wouldn't have killed her to go on a camping trip sometimes
      and
She says it wouldn't have killed him to put on the velvet
      smoking jacket she gave him for Christmas sometimes and
He thinks Marshall McLuhan is a fascist and
She thinks Richard and Pat Nixon have an unwholesome
      relationship and
He only likes paintings when you know what it's a painting of and
She only likes paintings when you don't.

June gets custody of the children
And Mark gets their dog, their orthodontia bills,
And visitation rights on alternate weekends, because
He thinks a great meal is shrimp cocktail and filet mignon and
She thinks a great meal is something like brains cooked in wine and
He says she is a fascist and
She says he and his mother have an unwholesome relationship and
He only likes women who'd rather make love than read Proust and
She only likes men who'd vice versa.

How come we thought they were such a perfect match?

Infidelity

In my burnt-orange Dynel lounging pajamas
With the rhinestone buttons,
I was, I concede, looking more abandoned than usual,
Which is probably the reason
Why my husband's best friend
Made overtures.

My pulse quickened,
And I could imagine . . .
    Cryptic conversations.
    Clandestine martinis.
    Tumultuous embraces.
    And me explaining
    That I can't slip away on Thursdays because of cub scouts.
    And that long kisses clog my sinuses.

Under the bridge table
His hand-sewn moccasins
Rubbed insistently against my Bernardo sandals,
While Dionne Warwick
Sang something suggestive
In stereo.

My lips trembled,
And I could imagine . . .
    Stolen weekends at a windswept beach.
    Waves pounding on the shore.
    And pounding on the door
    Of our motel hideaway,
    The Vice Squad.

Over the salt-free peanuts and diet soda
His contact lenses
Sought mine,
As I sucked in my stomach
And asked him,
Coffee or Sanka.

My throat tightened.
My lips trembled.
My pulse quickened . . .
    But aggravation
    Was all
    I could imagine.

The Generation Gap

Our sons are growing up
And any day now
They'll be sniffing glue,
Smoking pot,
Slipping LSD into their cream of wheat,
And never trusting anyone over thirty,
Even parents
Who once sang Foggy Foggy Dew
In youth hostels,
And Freiheit
In trench coats on the Fire Island ferry.

Our sons are growing up
And any day now
They'll be burning draft cards,
Doubting the Warren Commission,
Saying God is dead,
And never trusting anyone over thirty,
Even parents
Who once deplored prejudice
In petitions,
And capital punishment
In unpublished letters to the Times.

Our sons are growing up
And any day now
They'll be doing their own thing,
Telling it like it is,
Denouncing the military-industrial complex,
And never trusting anyone over thirty,
Even parents
Who tried agitation
Before they did,
And alienation
Before they did,
And once never trusted anyone
Over thirty.

69

True Love

It's true love because
I put on eyeliner and a concerto and make pungent observations
        about the great issues of the day
Even when there's no one here but him,
And because
I do not resent watching the Green Bay Packers
Even though I am philosophically opposed to football,
And because
When he is late for dinner and I know he must be either having an affair
        or lying dead in the middle of the street,
I always hope he's dead.

It's true love because
If he said quit drinking martinis but I kept drinking them and the
        next morning I couldn't get out of bed,
He wouldn't tell me he told me,
And because
He is willing to wear unironed undershorts
Out of respect for the fact that I am philosophically opposed to ironing,
And because
If his mother was drowning and I was drowning and he had to choose
        one of us to save,
He says he'd save me.

It's true love because
When he went to San Francisco on business while I had to stay home
        with the painters and the exterminator and the baby who was
        getting the chicken pox,
He understood why I hated him,
And because
When I said that playing the stock market was juvenile and irresponsible
        and then the stock I wouldn't let him buy went up twenty-six points,
I understood why he hated me,
And because
Despite cigarette cough, tooth decay, acid indigestion, dandruff, and
        other features of married life that tend to dampen the fires of
        passion,
We still feel something
We can call
True love.

71

About the Author

Judith Viorst's poems have appeared in New York Magazine, Holiday, and the Washingtonian. She is the author of The Village Square, and a juvenile, Sunday Morning, and has written articles for newspapers and magazines. Mrs. Viorst lives in Washington with her husband, the political writer Milton Viorst, and their sons, Anthony, Nicholas, and Alexander.